LITERATURE

INVESTIGATING MYSTERIES

SCHOLASTIC INC.

ISBN 0-590-49262-4

CONTENTS

THE CASE

OF THE

MISSING RING

by

DONALD J. SOBOL

Illustrated by

LEONARD SHORTALL

B ecause of Idaville's wonderful police record, Chief Brown was often asked to solve cases in other towns.

One evening he received a call to help the police of Ocean City. He took Encyclopedia with him.

"What is the case all about?" asked Encyclopedia, getting into the car beside his father.

"A ring is missing," answered Chief Brown. "Two masked men broke into the home of Mr. James Bevan last night. But no one, including Mr. Bevan, is sure the ring was stolen."

"How come?" said Encyclopedia.

"I didn't get all the facts over the telephone," replied Chief Brown. "But the mystery has to do with Mr.

Bevan himself. He lost his memory. He left a note, but he doesn't remember writing it."

Encyclopedia had never come up against anything like that. The half hour's drive seemed to take all night.

At last his father slowed the car and parked before a large house.

Chief Moore of the Ocean City police department appeared at the door.

"I'm glad you could come," he said. "This case has me going around in circles."

After shaking hands, he led Encyclopedia and his father into the study.

"The house belongs to Mr. James Bevan," he said. "The theft of the ring—if there was a theft—took place last night."

"What does the ring look like?" asked Chief Brown.

"It's a diamond ring," said Chief Moore. "It belonged to King Louis XIV of France. It's worth a fortune!"

Chief Moore pointed to a tiny glass box which lay on the desk beside a typewriter.

"Mr. Bevan kept the ring in the glass box to admire it," he said. "It was too small to fit his finger."

Then, for the next few minutes he told Chief Brown and Encyclopedia what he knew about the case. The facts were:

On the night of the theft, Mrs. Bevan had gone to a movie. Mr. Bevan had stayed home, for he needed a cane to get around and seldom went out.

About midnight the doorbell rang. Mr. Bevan, who was alone in the house, opened the door. Two masked men pushed their way inside. They demanded to know where the diamond ring was kept.

Mr. Bevan told them it was upstairs in his wife's jewelry case. He wanted time to hide the ring. As the men started upstairs, one of them hit him on the head with a gun.

"That's all Mr. Bevan can tell me," said Chief Moore. "I spoke with him this morning in the hospital. He can't remember a thing that happened between the time he was hit and the moment he woke up in the hospital."

"Did the two thieves steal Mrs. Bevan's jewels?" asked Chief Brown.

"Yes, but Mrs. Bevan says the whole lot isn't worth half of the diamond ring."

"Is there any clue to prove that Mr. Bevan, after he was hit on the head, hid the diamond ring so the thieves couldn't find it?" said Chief Brown.

"This typewritten note," said Chief Moore, taking a sheet of paper from his pocket. He showed it to Chief Brown and Encyclopedia. It read:

"Two men tried to steal the diamond ring. They hunted all over the house, raving about like madmen. They even split open the cat! When all failed, they beat me, but I didn't tell and so they hunted a little while longer. I may be dying. I hid the ring in the vane."

"If I understand the case so far," said Chief Brown, "Mr. Bevan wrote the note to his wife while the thieves searched the house. He feared he was dying from the beating and might not live to tell where he hid the diamond."

"Correct," said Chief Moore. "He must have put the note in a drawer of the desk after the thieves had searched it. Now he can't remember anything. He can't recall hiding the diamond ring or typing the note."

"Who found him?" asked Chief Brown.

"His wife—when she returned from the movie," said Chief Brown. "He was lying on the floor near the desk."

"Did you look for the ring in the vane?" asked Chief Brown. "The note says he hid it there."

"The only vane Mr. Bevan knows of is the weather vane on the roof," said Chief Moore. "I took it down. The ring wasn't inside it."

"What about the cat?"

"That part is the biggest mystery," said Chief Moore. "Why should thieves split open a cat, unless they thought the poor animal had swallowed the ring?"

"Did you find its body?" asked Chief Brown.

"No," answered Chief Moore. "Mr. Bevan never owned a cat. I suppose a cat must have got into the house somehow, and the thieves took no chances. They looked into everything. Why, they tore the house apart. Come with me."

He led Encyclopedia and Chief Brown down to the basement. It was in ruins. Everything was overturned. A large wooden barrel, or vat, had been split open. Wine from it spilled over the floor.

THE CASE OF THE MISSING RING

"This morning the rest of the house looked as bad," said Chief Moore. "Mrs. Bevan worked all day with the help of neighbors, straightening up."

"Perhaps the thieves did find the diamond ring," said Chief Brown. "They might have typed the note themselves to throw us off their trail."

"No, they didn't, Dad," whispered Encyclopedia. "The diamond ring is hidden in—"

WHERE?

Solution to The Case of the Missing Ring

Encyclopedia knew that Mr. Bevan had typed the word "cat" in his note by mistake.

Only the wood barrel, also called a vat, in the basement had been "split open." This was the clue.

The boy detective did not believe that Mr. Bevan, after being hit on the head and beaten up, could have typed the note without making a mistake.

Mr. Bevan's mistake, Encyclopedia saw, was that he had struck the letter "v" whenever he had meant to strike the letter "c." These letters are next to each other on a typewriter keyboard.

So Mr. Bevan had typed "cat" instead of "vat," "raving" instead of "racing." And when he wrote where he had hidden the ring, he had typed "vane" instead of "cane."

Thanks to Encyclopedia, the ring was found in Mr. Bevan's cane!

MEG MACKINTOSH
AND THE CASE OF THE
MISSING BABE RUTH BASEBALL

by

LUCINDA LANDON

"**H**mm, I do detect a bit of a family resemblance," said Meg Mackintosh, as she examined Gramps' old family photo album.

"You've got some funny-looking relatives," remarked Liddy. "And look at these pictures of you and Peter!"

Meg turned another page.

"Gramps, who's this?"

"That's me," explained Gramps, "and that's my cousin Alice. She was always bossing me around. She used to drive me crazy, teasing me about my little dog and calling me 'Georgie Porgie.' I called her 'Tattletale Al' because she was

always getting me in trouble.

"I'll never forget the day that photo was taken. We went on a picnic," Gramps reminisced. "That was the day she lost my prize possession."

"What was it?" Meg asked.

"My baseball, signed by the Babe himself."

"A baby signed your baseball?"

"Of course not. Babe Ruth, the greatest baseball player ever. He autographed the ball and gave it to my father and my father gave it to me. I took it to that picnic and Alice lost it. I never saw it again."

Meg examined the photo. Alice did look like a troublemaker. Then Meg spied something else.

The corner of a piece of paper was sticking out from behind the old photograph. Meg pulled it out and carefully unfolded it.

Dear Georgie Porgie,

August 1928

Summer is over, it went so fast,
Too bad your poison ivy had to last.
Sorry, I scared you in the hay.
What a pity your kitty ran away.
And the time you hated me most of all,
The day I lost your precious baseball!
Well here's a mystery, here's a clue,
Maybe I can make it up to you.
The answer could be with you right now,
But you wouldn't know it anyhow.

your cousin
Alice

Clue one—
Not a father
Not a gander
Take a look
In her book

"Hear that, Gramps? Maybe your baseball's not lost. Just follow the clue!" exclaimed Meg.

"I doubt it's that simple, Meg-O. Just another of her pranks. I saw that note years ago, but I couldn't make head or tail of it," Gramps sighed.

"It's probably too old to make sense now," added Liddy.

"But it might really mean something. I've got to investigate," insisted Meg.

Just then the phone rang.

"Hey, Nut-Meg, Peter here. Remind Gramps that I'll be there in the morning."

"Take your time. I've found a mystery. Something to do with a Babe Ruth baseball," Meg teased.

"A Babe Ruth baseball? That's worth a fortune! Don't touch anything until I get there!" shouted Peter.

"Tough luck, Sherlock, I can solve this one myself. Bye."

Upstairs in Gramps' boyhood room, where Meg always stayed, she took out her notebook and pencil.

"Finally. The chance I've been waiting for!" Meg told Liddy. "Peter won't let me join his Detective Club until I have 'proof' that I can solve a mystery."

"Well, you'd better do it before he gets here tomorrow," warned Liddy. "He'll never give you a chance."

Meg knew Liddy was right. She sat down at the desk and started a list.

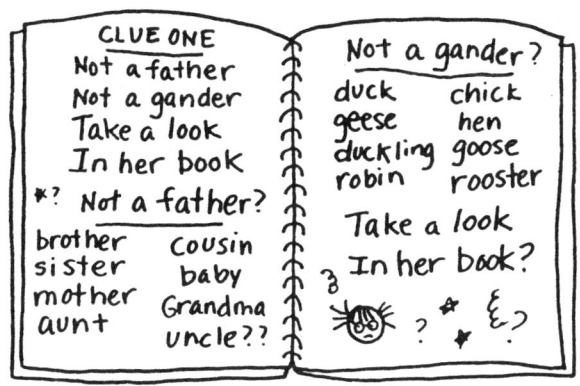

"Take a look in her book." Meg looked at the clue again. "Alice's diary? A nature book about birds?" She gazed up at the shelf of Gramps' old books.

"The Old Woman and the Little Red Hen," Liddy suggested as she squinted at the dusty titles. "Doesn't that fit?"

"I don't think so," said Meg, still jotting in her notebook. Suddenly she reached for a book. "I think I've got it!"

THE CASE OF THE MISSING BABE RUTH BASEBALL

WHICH BOOK DID MEG REACH FOR?

"Not a father, that's mother. Not a gander, that's goose. The Mother Goose book!" Meg explained. She carefully opened it.

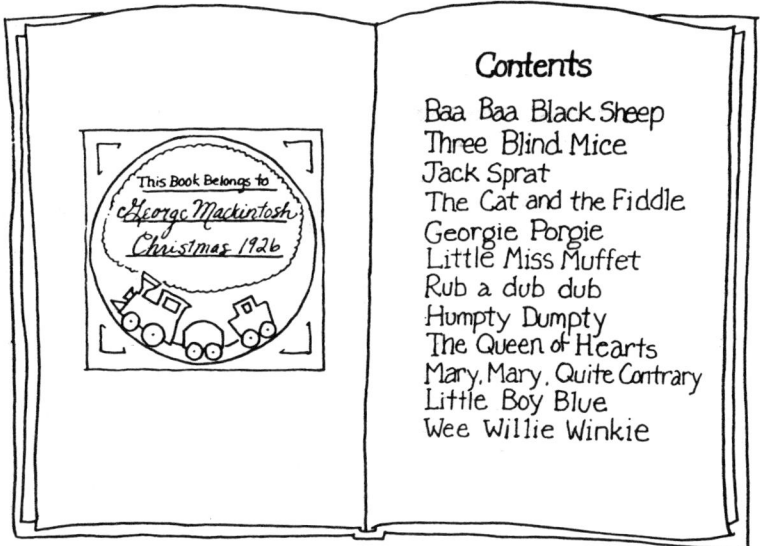

Contents

Baa Baa Black Sheep
Three Blind Mice
Jack Sprat
The Cat and the Fiddle
Georgie Porgie
Little Miss Muffet
Rub a dub dub
Humpty Dumpty
The Queen of Hearts
Mary, Mary, Quite Contrary
Little Boy Blue
Wee Willie Winkie

This Book Belongs to George Mackintosh Christmas 1926

"This is definitely Gramps' old book. We must be on the right track," Meg said. After a moment she added, "I think I know where to look."

WHICH RHYME DID MEG TURN TO?

"Georgie Porgie, pudding and pie . . ." said Meg.
"Kissed the girls and made them cry . . ." added Liddy as she twirled a pencil in her hair. "So?"
"Georgie Porgie. That's what Alice called Gramps," Meg reminded her. Sure enough there was a small note tucked tightly between the pages. Another clue!

"Little boy blue, come blow your horn," Meg recited.

"But what does a horn have to do with a baseball?" wondered Liddy.

"I don't know yet. First we have to find a horn. Let's see. Foghorn? Cow horn? Horn of plenty? Cape Horn?"

Clue two
Little boy blue
with the cows
in the corn
Whatever you do
Don't blow this ?

"Well, good luck with it. I have to get home," Liddy said.

Meg walked Liddy downstairs, then went to find Gramps.

"Gramps, did you ever play any musical instrument, like a French horn?"

"No, but I can sing a little. Why?" Gramps replied.

"I found another clue. Alice hid it in your old Mother Goose book, on the Georgie Porgie page. It has something to do with a horn."

"That's easy." Gramps grinned as he pointed to the bookshelf. Meg followed his finger to the old bugle there. She took it down to inspect it. She removed the mouthpiece, shook it, and peered inside with her flashlight. But no clue.

Gramps got up from the couch. "Well, my dear detective, it's time to turn in. I wouldn't get my hopes up over these clues. Old Alice, she was a sly one."

"Maybe this isn't going to be as easy as I thought," Meg whispered to Skip as they went upstairs to bed.

Meg checked her detective kit. Everything was in order—a magnifying glass, a pair of tweezers to pick up small clues, flashlight and extra batteries, tape measure, scissors, envelopes, and, of course, her detective notebook and pencils.

"I have to be sure to write everything down," she said to Skip as she got under the covers. "The tiniest fact can solve the biggest mystery. Track, write, decode, deduce . . . then I'll have plenty of proof to show Peter and his Detective Club." After a while she slid her notebook under her pillow and dozed off to sleep.

"Yikes," shrieked Meg. "Stop! Please stop that awful noise!"

Gramps put the bugle down. "If you think that's bad, Meg-O, you should have heard your father play it. I got this bugle for him when he went to Scout Camp. He was a pitiful horn player. Ah well, rise and shine for breakfast."

When Meg got downstairs, Gramps was making pancakes. "All this talk about Alice reminds me of when we were kids. Once she challenged me to a pancake-eating contest. I ate sixteen, while she watched with a miserable grin on her face. When it was her turn she ate three and forfeited the contest. She had decided from the start to let me win. All I won was a stomachache!" Gramps laughed. "Alice was always getting the best of me."

But Meg was only half listening. She was still puzzled over something Gramps had said earlier. Something had to be wrong with the horn clue.

INVESTIGATING MYSTERIES

WHAT WAS IT?

"Wait a minute!" Meg shouted. "Gramps, if you got this bugle for Dad when he was a kid, it couldn't be the right horn. It wasn't even around when Alice drummed up this whole mystery."

"Guess that's so," Gramps admitted sheepishly.

Meg looked at the clue again. "Whatever you do, don't blow this horn." Remembering another kind of horn, she raced into the living room.

"You wouldn't want to blow this horn, eh, Skip," Meg said as she took the old powder horn off the hook. She pulled off the cap. There was no powder inside, but there was something else. Meg took her tweezers out of her detective kit and slowly pulled out a small, tightly rolled piece of paper.

"I guess I'm not surprised that nobody has looked in there lately," said Gramps. "Maybe you really are onto something, Meg-O. What does it say?"

> ucle reeth
> tillet ob epep
> stol reh ?

"I don't know. Does it mean anything to you, Gramps?"

"Never cared much for word puzzles myself," confessed Gramps, "but if you find one of those jigsaw puzzles with the pictures, I'll be glad to help you."

Meg shook her head and sighed. Peter would be arriving soon. She had to solve this mystery fast. Just then the back door slammed and Meg jumped.

"Whew, it's only you," Meg said with a sigh as Liddy came into the room.

"Only me? Only me might help you solve this," Liddy replied as she read the clue. "It looks like a secret-alphabet code. You know, when each letter stands for a different letter in the alphabet."

"Or maybe the letters in each word are just scrambled around," said Meg. She took out her notebook and began trying different combinations.

Before long the door slammed again. Peter was peering over their shoulders.

"Here's a clue for you, Nut-Meg: Drop it!" Peter said. "I can have this solved in no time!"

"I found it, I followed it, and I'll finish it," protested Meg, covering her notes. But not quickly enough.

"What's this? A word puzzle? I could put it on my computer and have it decoded in a flash," Peter persisted. "What's it got to do with a Babe Ruth baseball, anyway?"

Meg snatched the clue back. "Don't bother. I've already figured it out with my own brainpower!"

AND SHE HAD. HAVE YOU?

"Well, what does it say?" asked Liddy, as Peter stomped out of the room. "I counted seven E's, but what does that mean?"

"Nothing. It's not an alphabet code. It is a scrambled-letter code. The letters in each word are just mixed around."

"It says: 'Clue three little bo peep lost her'—her sheep, of course," said Meg.

"Why didn't I see that?" said Liddy, shutting the dictionary.

"Is it something to do with sheep's wool, or an old spinning wheel?" wondered Meg.

"Or a sheepskin?" suggested Liddy.

Meg and Liddy looked high and low. Meanwhile, Peter was eagerly searching the old photo albums, jotting down notes. He was more nerve-racking than Alice and her crazy clues, thought Meg.

It wasn't until later in the afternoon, when Liddy had gone home, that Meg realized what the answer to the sheep clue was.

DO YOU KNOW WHERE BO PEEP'S LOST SHEEP CAN BE FOUND?

"Right in front of me all along," Meg sighed. She carefully unhooked the old painting. On the back, tucked tightly between the canvas and the frame, was another small note. But it had crumbled over time.

Meg wrote down what she could decipher. "Aha! Another scrambled code," said Peter, and Meg jumped. She hadn't heard him come up behind her. "Wait until the guys see that baseball!"

"Stay out of this! You don't even know what it's all about," Meg answered. "Anyway, it's Gramps' baseball."

"I think I've got it unjumbled . . . B-U-D-D-H-A!" Peter raced to the statue in the living room.

But Meg knew he was wasting his time. Taking her notes with her, she slipped off to find the answer to the clue.

WHAT DID THE CLUE MEAN AND WHERE DID MEG LOOK?

Peter was way off. It wasn't a scrambled-letter code at all. It was a line from another Mother Goose rhyme. Alice must have meant tub.

Meg was scouring the bathroom for clues when Gramps leaned in the door. "Sorry to disappoint you, Meg-O, but you won't find much here. You see, it's like the horn. This bathroom isn't as old as those clues."

"A new bathroom? Then where's the old one?" asked Meg.

"Well, we put a bathroom in the house, but we didn't take one out, so to speak. Back when I was a youngster, we just had an outhouse. We took baths in an old tub in the kitchen," Gramps said.

"This can't be a dead end," sighed Meg. "There's got to be a solution after I've gotten this far."

THE CASE OF THE MISSING BABE RUTH BASEBALL

"Alice was cunning," Gramps said.
Meg had to agree.

Later that night, Peter knocked on Meg's door. "Are
you still sleeping with Gramps' old stuffed animals? A
little babyish don't you think? I gave up that pathetic
old dog years ago."

"What do you really want, Peter?" Meg said suspi-
ciously.

"Hey, Meggy, let's put our heads together on this
mystery. I could help you out. For instance, the old
outhouse, where Gramps keeps his gardening stuff
now. I bet that has something to do with it. Well, see ya
in the morning, Nut-Meg."

"I'd already thought of that," Meg said to herself,
"but I'd better not wait around until tomorrow to
check it out. Peter might get there first." When she
thought that Gramps and Peter were safely asleep, she
pulled her raincoat and boots over her pajamas and tiptoed outside. The air was cool and the ground was still
damp from the rain. Meg flicked
on her flashlight and headed for
the rickety old toolshed.

The flimsy door swung open.
Meg spied a pile of tools and
flowerpots and an old rain barrel.
Was it an old washtub? It must
be—there was a note wedged
betweeen the wooden slats! She
pulled it out and opened it up.

But instead of reaching for the shovel, Meg sat back on her heels and thought. There was something funny about this clue.

HOW DID MEG KNOW?
HINT: THERE ARE FIVE TELLTALE SIGNS
CAN YOU SPOT THEM ALL?

1. It was on lined paper. All the other clues were on unlined.
2. It was ripped out of a spiral notebook. None of the other were.
3. The handwriting slanted to the left. Alice's slanted to the right.
4. It said "Clue #4"—but Meg had already found the fourth clue.
5. It had nothing to do with Mother Goose rhymes.

Clearly, this was a fake clue. Someone was trying to throw her off the track. Meg was sure she knew who . . . and after looking around the tool shed again, she knew where.

Someone had been here recently. There were fresh muddy footprints and the dust marks showed that the cabinet had been emptied. Ten to one, Peter was inside.

Meg picked up the shovel and scraped it around on the floor, pretending to dig. After a moment, she came up with the perfect plan to turn the tables on Peter.

"Yikes!" she said loudly. "Spiders—a whole nest of them! Come on, Skip, let's split!" She slammed the toolshed door behind her, then tiptoed around the side and peered through the window. In a flash, Peter tumbled out of the cabinet and bolted back to the house.

Meg held her breath to keep from laughing. "I'm not scared of spiders," she said to herself, "but you-know-who is . . . Mr. Big-Shot Detective! It serves him right for leaving that careless clue."

But, as she headed back to bed, she had to admit she was still no further along in solving the mystery. And time was running out. Mom and Dad would be picking them up the next day at noon.

In the morning, Gramps asked Meg to get some kindling for the wood cookstove. He kept it in a funny-shaped metal bin. The old bathtub!

Meg searched the old tub for a clue, but there was no note, not a scrap of paper.

"Rats! How else could Alice have left a clue?" wondered Meg as she stirred figure eights in her oatmeal. Gramps always gave her huge spoons. This one had a fancy M engraved on it.

As Meg stared at the spoon, she suddenly had an idea of how a message could have been left.

Just as she suspected, there was something scratched on the bottom of the tub.

"Another clue!" Meg exclaimed. This one looked too authentic to be one of Peter's tricks.

"Gramps, did you have any dogs when you were little?" Meg asked.

"Oh, yes," he replied, "probably a dozen or so. Let's see, there was Nippy and Nicky and Lucky and Flippy and twice as many cats. Gosh, we had a lot of pets—ducks, pigs, ponies, even a parrot."

Then the phone rang. It was Liddy.

"What's happening with the mystery?" she asked.

"Can't talk now," Meg whispered as she noticed Peter at the top of the stairs.

"Is that Lydia-the-Encyclopedia on the phone? Tell her I've got this case just about wrapped up," Peter said as he came down the stairs and glanced over Meg's shoulder. "So what's the latest clue?"

"It has something to do with little Miss Muffett," Meg teased, "and the spider that sat down beside her, you know, scaring Miss Muffett away?"

"What are you talking about?" said Liddy. "Whatever you do, don't let him get it."

"Don't worry, he's bluffing." Meg hung up. She hoped she was right and that this wasn't all a wild-goose chase. She had some deducing of her own to do—fast. Her only hope was to go back to the beginning.

Meg studied the old clues, then looked at the new one. " 'The little dog laughed.' If I'm right, it's part of a Mother Goose rhyme, too. And I think I know which one."

WHICH NURSERY RHYME WAS IT?

Meg found the rhyme in Gramps' Mother Goose book.

Deductions
1) All clues have to do with Mother Goose rhymes.

2) All clues are hidden in this house.

3) Clues can only be found in old things because Alice hid them long ago.

"This could lead any-where! Cat, fiddle, cow, moon, dish, spoon?" Meg tried not to panic. She took out the old photo of Gramps and Alice that had started her on this investi-gation and reread Alice's letter and clues.

The Cat and the Fiddle

Hey, diddle, diddle!
The cat and the fiddle,
The cow jumped over the moon,
The little dog laughed
To see such sport,
And the dish ran away with the spoon.

Peter had been upstairs and down, rummaging through all sorts of stuff. Was he really onto some-thing and was she the one off the track?

Meg was determined to solve the mystery. And as she stared at the photo and clue, it all fell into place.

WHAT WAS THE ANSWER?

Meg ran into her bedroom. Safely tucked under the covers was the old stuffed animal that had once belonged to Gramps. The old toy dog. It was the same one that was in the photograph, the one Peter had teased Meg about.

"The little dog laughed," Meg said to herself. "Of course! 'The answer could be with you right now, but you wouldn't know it anyhow' . . . just as Alice said in the letter."

Meg looked at the old toy intently. He was musty and worn. His body was very hard, stuffed with straw.

On his back was a loose thread. It was a different color, as if someone had tried to mend a seam but hadn't done a very good job.

Meg carefully pulled the thread. Sure enough, deep inside the straw was something you'd never expect to find in an old doggie doll.

The baseball. Just as she had hoped! There was one final note with it, but Meg decided to let Gramps read it.

"What's this?" He woke with a start. "I must be dreaming. My baseball? It couldn't be!"

"It is," said Meg.

"It's what?" Peter burst in.

"It's my Babe Ruth baseball, long lost, and now Meg has found it," Gramps said with a grin.

"That's right," said Meg. "Alice hid the ball in your old toy dog. With all that hard stuffing, no one ever noticed. She left the Mother Goose clues to help you track it down."

"Amazing," said Gramps.

"Amazing all right," grumbled Peter. "She just got lucky fooling around with those old baby toys."

"Sometimes he reminds me of someone, but I don't know who." Gramps winked at Meg.

"Maybe this will help you remember. It's a note from you-know-who," Meg said, winking back.

August 1928

Dear Georgie Porgie Pudding and Pie,
  This time I really made you cry.
Your baseball was never lost it's true,
But I didn't know how to give it back to you.
I thought a mystery would be fun,
  With some little clues —
    To keep you on the run!
                          your cousin
                            Alice

P.S. I hope it doesn't take
  you _too_ long to find it.

"Not too long," said Gramps. "Only over fifty years! Wait until I call her and tell her the game is up! And Peter, you be sure to tell everybody back at the Detective Club how Meg-O the supersleuth cracked the case."

Peter groaned. "Oh, all right." Then he even smiled a little.

They heard Mom and Dad's car pull into the driveway. "And solved not a moment too soon," Meg said as she hugged Gramps good-bye.

"You'd better take this along for 'proof,' " Gramps replied, tossing her the baseball.

"Did you catch that, Peter?" Meg laughed. "Wait till the Detective Club sees this!"

THE BINNACLE BOY

by

PAUL FLEISCHMAN

Illustrated by

ILENE WINN-LEDERER

1

When the brig *Orion*, three weeks out from Havana, appeared off her home port of New Bethany, Maine, Miss Evangeline Frye was just parting her bed curtains, formally banishing night.

While those who'd chanced to spy the sails wondered why the ship hadn't fired a salute, Miss Frye was combing her coarse, gray hair. While the *Orion* drifted unexpectedly about, at last presenting her stern to the harbor, Miss Frye was blowing the hearth fire into being. And while the harbor pilot's drowsy son rowed his father out to the ship, to return in a frenzy, eyes wide and hands trembling, Miss Frye was stationed at her parlor window, awaiting the sight of Sarah Peel.

She peered down the length of Bartholomew Street. Straight-spined as a mast and so tall that her gaze was aimed out through the top row of windowpanes, Miss

Frye eyed the clock on the town hall next door. It was eight fifteen. The girl was late—and plenty of scrubbing and spinning to be done.

She pursed her lips, lowered her eyes, and looked out upon her flower garden. It was nearly Independence Day—tansy was thriving, pinks were in bloom, marigolds were budding on schedule. But the poppy seeds she'd bought from a rogue of a peddler, and gullibly planted with care, still hadn't sent up a single shoot. And probably never would, she reflected. In memory, she heard her mother's voice: "Girls take after their mothers, Evangeline. Men take after the Devil." She regarded the bare stretch of soil below, sneering at this latest confirmation.

The door knocker sounded. Miss Frye opened up and was surprised to find not Sarah Peel, but her ten-year-old younger sister, Tekoa.

"I've come to do chores, ma'am."

Miss Frye cocked her head. "But where is Sarah?"

"In bed, ma'am. Taken ill." The girl spoke softly, tucking a strand of straw-blond hair under her kerchief.

"Well then." Miss Frye motioned her in and closed the door behind her. "I suppose you've had practice scouring pewter."

Tekoa stood in the hallway, silent.

Miss Frye blinked her eyes. Was this some impertinence? Then at once she recalled what Sarah had told her—that the girl had been left deaf by a fever and was able to listen only with her eyes, by reading the words on others' lips.

Miss Frye passed Tekoa, then turned to face her. "You can begin with the pewter."

"Yes, ma'am," said the girl.

Miss Frye led her down the hall to the kitchen. "And what manner of illness has seized poor Sarah?"

"Her jaws," said Tekoa. "They won't come open."

Miss Frye appeared startled. "And when did this happen?"

"This morning, just after the news of the *Orion*."

Miss Frye's eyebrows jerked. "The *Orion*? What news?" Among the crew of New Bethany boys was Miss Frye's adopted son, Ethan.

"She appeared offshore this morning, ma'am," Tekoa calmly replied.

At once Miss Frye rushed to the window.

"All of the crew were found to be dead."

2

Bells were tolled. Trunks were opened and mourning clothes solemnly exhumed. The crew of the brig *Orion* was buried. And yet the matter remained unfinished.

No evidence of attack had been found. There was no sign of scurvy, no shortage of food. When the ship was boarded the crew was discovered to be lying about the decks as if hexed, with no witness to bear the tale to the living. None, that is, except the binnacle boy.

He alone remained standing, the life-sized carving of a sailor boy holding the iron binnacle, the housing for the ship's compass. Straight backed, sober lipped, in his jacket and cap, he stood resolutely before the helm, his lacquered eyes shining chicory blue. And after the ship's sails had been furled and her cargo of molasses unloaded, the binnacle boy was laid in a wagon and, like the seventeen sailors before him, slowly borne up the road to the top of the cliff upon which New Bethany stood. And there, before the town hall, the pinewood statue was mounted, still bearing the ship's compass, a memorial to the *Orion*'s crew.

Upon him the families of the dead gazed for hours, convinced he'd somehow reveal the nature of the catastrophe he'd witnessed. Mothers kept watch on his ruddy lips, expecting each moment to see them move. Fathers stared into his painted eyes, waiting to catch them in the act of blinking. Children cocked their ears to the wind as it moaned eerily over the boy, and believed they heard the sound of his voice.

Yet the binnacle boy clung to his secret. The mystery of the *Orion* remained, and gradually, as the summer progressed, those who stood and awaited the boy's words were replaced by those who'd come instead to leave him with secrets of their own, knowing his steadfast lips to be sealed.

At first it was children who took up the practice. After whispering into his chiseled ear, they ran off, or studied his stouthearted features as if expecting a nod of acknowledgment. Soon their elders took after them, and before long the binnacle boy became the repository for all that couldn't be safely spoken aloud in New Bethany.

Lovers opened their hearts to him. Hurrying figures sought him out in the night. Those who felt their lives running out entrusted him with their final confessions.

It was one of these last, a long-winded farmer, whom Miss Frye was observing from her parlor one morning when she noticed three women with parasols filing down the walk toward her door.

"Tekoa," she addressed her helper. "I believe we have company."

The brass door knocker sounded three times. Tekoa set down her feather duster, opened the door, and showed into the parlor Miss Bunch, Miss Mayhew, and Mrs. Stiggins.

"Good day to you, Miss Frye," chirped Miss Bunch. Without asking, she plopped herself down on a chair, a trespass that drew a stare from her hostess. Affirming her sovereign powers, Miss Frye regally motioned the others to be seated.

"It's some time since you've been seen about," said Miss Bunch. "So we decided to come on our own." She dabbed at the sweat on her brow with a handkerchief, adjusted her bonnet, and opened her fan. "To express our condolences, that is. About your son, Ethan."

"Indeed," said Miss Mayhew.

"You're very kind," replied Miss Frye. She noted that, like herself, Mrs. Stiggins was attired in a black mourning dress.

"I believe that your Ethan and my Jeroboam were dear companions," Mrs. Stiggins spoke up. "Aye, and full of mischief, as well."

THE BINNACLE BOY

"All boys be apprenticed to the Devil," said Miss
Frye.

Tekoa entered with a pitcher of cider.

"And tell me, child," Miss Bunch addressed her.
"How does your sister Sarah progress?"

"She's able to open her mouth, ma'am, and eat. But
she's weak still, and refuses to speak to a soul."

"Truly now!" Miss Bunch lamented. "Come, child—
sit down and visit with us."

Tekoa turned her eyes toward her mistress, who was
glaring across at Miss Bunch in dismay.

"If you're fully caught up with your work," said Miss
Frye, "you may take a chair, Tekoa, and join us."

The girl found herself a seat in the corner. And in
the midst of the conversation Miss Bunch noticed
Tekoa looking out the window.

She touched the girl's shoulder. "What do you see,
child?"

"Excuse me, ma'am. Nothing of importance,
ma'am."

"Nothing?" Miss Bunch lowered her voice. "You
were eyeing the binnacle boy, I warrant. Watching the
ones that speak in his ear—same as I'd be doing myself
if I knew the trick of reading lips." She glanced at Miss
Mayhew and the two traded smiles.

"In truth, I was watching the swallows, ma'am."

"Swallows!" Miss Bunch commenced to chuckle.
"Any fool can see swallows, child. But perhaps you'd
put your eyes to use—and tell us what you next see spoken into the statue's ear."

Miss Mayhew's own dim eyes lit up.

"Really!" protested Miss Frye. "That's not proper!"

"Purely to help pass the time," said Miss Bunch. "To take our minds from our grief for a spell."

Tekoa stared at the women uneasily.

"And naturally," Miss Mayhew piped up, "with the curtains drawn, only she'll know who's speaking."

"And she'll not disclose the name," Miss Bunch added.

Miss Frye looked over at Mrs. Stiggins. Both knew that the matter wasn't right. And yet they too were curious as to what was said to the binnacle boy. After all, they themselves wouldn't actually be eavesdropping. And the name of the speaker would remain a mystery, never to be revealed.

"You may humor Miss Bunch's wishes, Tekoa," Miss Frye announced after deliberation.

"Yes, ma'am," said the girl.

The curtains were closed, dimming the light. Tekoa reluctantly took up her post, while Miss Bunch and Miss Mayhew looked on in suspense.

The church bell declared it to be eleven. Then noon. Impatiently the women fanned themselves, squirming about like children in church. Then suddenly Tekoa drew back from the window.

"Did you spy someone?" Miss Bunch burst out. And suddenly it occurred to her that some sharp-eyed soul might reveal the fact that one of the various false teeth she wore had originally belonged to a dog.

"Yes, ma'am, I did."

Miss Mayhew grinned eagerly. "Well then—and what was spoken, child?"

The girl swallowed.

"Come now—speak up! Let us hear it word for word."

"Yes, ma'am."

Tekoa lowered her gaze. She studied her hands, and breathed in deeply.

" 'I know what killed the *Orion*'s crew.' "

3

After her three visitors had gone and Tekoa had finished her chores and left, Miss Frye climbed to the top of the stairs, and then, as she hadn't in weeks, turned right. Tekoa's revelation still rang in her head as she walked down the hall, came to a halt—and opened the door to Ethan's room.

She stood there in the doorway a moment. The room was musty, the light dim. She passed his bed, opened the curtains, and gazed out his window at the indigo sea, musing on all he might have been.

Miss Frye turned around. Surveying the cobwebs, she recalled that both her natural sons had occupied the room as well. But they'd grown up wild, and long ago had left, following their father to sea, and like him gaining a fondness for the rum they freighted across the waters. When the schooner on which all three had shipped went down in a gale off the Georgia coast, Miss Frye had been neither surprised nor sorry, and had returned with relief to her maiden name. Her mother, herself abandoned by her husband, regarded the sinking as a fitting judgment. "Men," she'd summed up, "are a stench in God's nostrils."

Miss Frye paced slowly about the room. She found herself staring at Ethan's washstand, recalling the chill October day she'd gone mushroom picking, miles from home, and discovered an infant wrapped in a flour sack, left at a crossroad, dead. Or so she'd feared, till she'd gradually warmed him, holding the bundle next to her skin—and felt him slowly begin to squirm. Astonished, she hadn't known what to do, until suddenly something her mother had long ago told her leaped into memory: "If you save a creature's life, Evangeline, you're responsible for its every deed afterward." Unwilling to entrust his raising to another, she'd borne him home, burnt the flour sack, bathed him thoroughly, and named him Ethan.

Miss Frye walked up to his mahogany desk. The lamp by which he'd worked was dusty. His goose quill pen and his ink bottle waited. She opened the primer he'd used, and recalled the pleasures of shaping his youthful mind.

A freethinker in religious matters, she'd refused to take the child to church and had taught him a catechism of her own devising. Shunning New Bethany's public school, Miss Frye had been his only tutor as well. She'd vowed that Ethan would turn out a gentleman, cultured and refined, an exception to his sex. No weed would be allowed to take root in the boy, no unwanted notion would enter his head. She would tend the child like a seedling tree, encouraging one branch and cutting another, keeping the image of its final shape fixed firmly in her mind. After all, she reasoned, God had meant him to die; by granting him life she'd assumed His role. The boy was thenceforward her private domain, whose growing body she marveled at as if it were her own work.

Tekoa's words came suddenly to mind and Miss Frye emerged from her reverie. She closed the curtains, shut the door, and marched downstairs to the parlor again.

It was dusk. She stood watch on the binnacle boy, hoping to catch someone seeking his ear, desperate to know whom Tekoa had seen.

When the light at last failed she gave up her vigil and slowly sipped down a bowl of bean soup. She wondered if Tekoa might have made up the message she'd reported—then quickly put the thought out of her head. There wasn't a speck of deceit in the girl, and Miss Frye wondered what Tekoa must think of a mistress who ordered her to eavesdrop.

She broke through the crust of a cold plum tart and considered the girl's ways. She performed her duties competently enough, and yet there was something distant about her. The others had hopped to Miss Frye's commands and striven anxiously to please her. They'd always been afraid of her, as Tekoa's sister Sarah had been—little wonder, since of all the town, Miss Frye alone did not go to church. She rarely went out, and was rarely visited. Yet in her presence quiet Tekoa seemed to be calmly detached.

Hoping to break through the girl's silence, and frantic to know whom she'd seen at the statue, she called Tekoa from her work the next morning and set her to watching the binnacle boy. She felt a need to win the girl to her and hoped she was appreciative of this respite from her chores. Doggedly, she attempted to kindle a conversation with the girl, in vain. Thereafter Miss Frye sat in silence, studying Tekoa's pale features, hoping the speaker she'd seen might return.

For an hour Tekoa watched from the window. Then glancing over to her left she sighted Miss Bunch and her companions, traveling under the portable shade of their parasols, bustling down the walk.

"Dear child—how good to see you," Miss Bunch addressed Tekoa at the door. "And good day to you as well, Miss Frye. As you're no doubt lonely without your dear son, we felt it to be our solemn duty to lend you our company once again."

"You're most kind," Miss Frye curtly replied.

"And while we're here," Miss Mayhew added, while Miss Frye led them into the parlor, "we thought Tekoa might be allowed to read out the secrets spoken to the statue."

"In quest of the truth concerning the *Orion*," Mrs. Stiggins sternly declared.

Miss Frye declined to mention the fact that she'd already had the girl doing just that. Ashamed to engage in the practice so openly, she decided to set Tekoa to spinning—when she glimpsed a woman crossing the street and heading toward the binnacle boy.

"Yes, of course!" she stammered. "Why—we owe it to the town!"

She hurried Tekoa back to her seat. A few moments later the girl turned around.

"Well?" asked Miss Frye. "Have you something to report?"

"Yes, ma'am," the girl gravely replied.

Mrs. Stiggins leaned forward. "Let us hear it, then, child!"

Tekoa lowered her eyes in embarrassment. " 'Miss Pike put no money in the collection plate at church, but only rattled the coins.' "

Miss Bunch and Miss Mayhew gaped at each other. A blush spread over Mrs. Stiggins.

"You may return to the window now, Tekoa," Miss Frye informed the girl.

In silence, the women fanned themselves. Mrs. Stiggins looked across at Miss Frye.

"My dear Jeroboam always spoke most highly of your Ethan."

Miss Frye gazed blankly, lost in thought. "He might have been a scholar. Or a poet, perhaps."

Slowly, Tekoa drew back from the window.

Miss Frye's eyes flashed.

"What is it? Something spoken?"

"Yes, ma'am."

"Well then—speak it out, Tekoa!"

The girl glanced down at the hardwood floor.

" 'Tonight we meet. Under the elm tree.' "

Miss Bunch gasped for breath. "Which elm tree, child?"

"Didn't say, ma'am," Tekoa replied.

Miss Bunch and Miss Mayhew sighed in unison. Again they waited while Tekoa watched.

"My Jeroboam had just turned fourteen," Mrs. Stiggins said. "And your Ethan?"

"Fourteen as well," Miss Frye replied.

Mrs. Stiggins released a sigh.

An hour passed. The church bell rang twelve. Miss Bunch yawned and reached for her parasol.

"Perhaps we should go."

"Indeed," said Miss Mayhew.

Suddenly, Tekoa turned. Her eyes appeared glazed, her features stiff.

"What is it?" Miss Frye demanded. "A message?"

"Yes, ma'am," the girl reluctantly replied.

"Gracious sakes, child—let us hear it then!"

Tekoa swallowed. She gazed absently before her.

" 'One of the tins of tea snuck among the *Orion*'s provisions—was poisoned.' "

"Poisoned?" shrieked Mrs. Stiggins. "The tea?"

Miss Frye jumped up. "Is there more, Tekoa?"

"That's all of it, ma'am."

Mrs. Stiggins shot forward. "I insist you reveal the speaker," she cried, taking hold of Tekoa's shoulders.

"But ma'am, the agreement—"

"She's right," said Miss Bunch. "The name of the speaker must not be revealed."

"But my very own Jeroboam—poisoned! The murderer must be brought to justice!"

"Perhaps," said Miss Mayhew, "the speaker is lying."

Slowly, Miss Frye paced the room. "But why would someone lie to the statue?"

"No reason at all," Mrs. Stiggins snapped. She sat back down and wrung her hands. "They must have opened the tea that morning."

"And Lord knows," Miss Mayhew grimly continued, "with all the molasses they sweeten it with, they might have drunk hemlock itself and not known it."

A silence fell over Miss Frye's three visitors. They rose to their feet, bid farewell to Miss Frye, and slowly retraced their steps down the street, avoiding the binnacle boy's eyes in passing, as if this knower of secrets might discover their own with a glance.

4

Miss Frye did not sleep well that night. The next morning Tekoa's revelation still echoed in her ears. When the girl arrived at eight o'clock, Miss Frye set her to mixing up bread dough and stepped outside to the garden.

At a deliberate pace she strolled the paths, searching for comfort in the company of flowers. She smiled to see her larkspur thriving, and lad's-love blooming in its appointed season. She gazed upon her Queen Margrets and mint, and sampled the various scents of her roses.

Sitting on a bench, she inspected her tansy, eyeing

the cornmeal-yellow petals and recalling how Ethan too had loved flowers. She grinned to remember the morning they'd merrily roamed the cliff, two summers before, collecting posies of hawkweed and chicory—and at once the smile left her lips. For that was the day the loquacious Mrs. Gump had stopped them to chat on their return. The woman's ill-mannered son had appeared, while she jabbered about her watery eye, and the pain in her lungs, and the history of her limp—till Miss Frye turned around to find the boys gone, dashing through Mrs. Gump's melon patch and trampling her corn, playing at pirates.

It was not till weeks later that Miss Frye discovered that Ethan was sneaking off in the evenings, to cavort with Mrs. Gump's son and others. When she'd confronted him he was unrepentant and had openly mocked her in Sarah's presence. Recalling her ship-bred, rum-sodden sons, she'd had no choice but to be stern with the boy, determined he'd bloom according to plan.

And now, she reflected, Ethan was gone, his promise lost forever.

Miss Frye marched indoors and entered the parlor, closed the curtains, and approached Tekoa. The girl was setting her dough to rise, and although Miss Frye knew there was mending to be done, she felt driven to find out if anything further about the *Orion* might come to light.

"Rest yourself awhile," said Miss Frye, "and aim your eyes on the binnacle boy."

The girl sat down and no sooner looked out than

Miss Bunch, Miss Mayhew, and Mrs. Stiggins made their way to the door.

"Good day, Tekoa," bubbled Miss Bunch. "And good day to you, my dear Miss Frye. A day especially long for one so recently robbed of her child."

"Indeed," said Miss Mayhew. "The very reason we felt bound to help you pass the time."

Miss Frye's lips puckered. "How very thoughtful."

"Perhaps Tekoa could be of assistance," suggested Miss Bunch.

"If she's free," said Miss Mayhew.

Mrs. Stiggins tapped her parasol on the floor. "That justice might be done."

The women seated themselves in the parlor and Tekoa resumed her place at the window.

An hour passed in silent suspense, Miss Frye's three guests providing the barest minimum of their promised companionship.

"Tell me, Tekoa," Miss Bunch spoke up. "How does your precious sister fare?"

"The same, ma'am," the girl replied.

Miss Bunch shook her head and softened her voice. "I've heard it said that Sarah had a sweetheart among the *Orion*'s crew. Simeon Sprigg, they say it was." She glanced from one pair of eyes to the next. "They say the two were seen talking together, and that he's the cause of the girl's affliction."

Her listeners shook their heads in sympathy, then returned their attention once more to Tekoa.

Patiently, the girl looked out, though no one was

near the binnacle boy. She trained her gaze on the swirling swallows and watched the swifts career through the sky. She studied a sparrow feeding its young—and suddenly noticed a figure appear, approach the statue, and seek out its ear.

"What is it, Tekoa?" Miss Frye demanded.

"Something spoken, ma'am. To the binnacle boy."

"Naturally, child! But what? Speak it out!"

Tekoa swallowed. She glanced about. Her lips quivered nervously.

" 'He wouldn't listen. He wished to roam free—and signed himself aboard the *Orion*.' "

Mrs. Stiggins bolted to her feet. "Quick, child—is this the same speaker as before?"

Gloomily, Tekoa nodded, and Mrs. Stiggins' eyes blazed.

"I demand to know who it is at once!"

Seeing the woman charging toward her, Tekoa clasped the curtains shut.

"Away, child!" Mrs. Stiggins ordered, as she grabbed a curtain—and flung it open.

"Sarah!" she gasped. "Sarah Peel!"

The others scrambled at once to the window.

"Protecting her older sister, she was!" Mrs. Stiggins shouted out. "But we'll get to the truth—believe me we will!"

Snatching her parasol, she steamed out the door, with Miss Bunch and Miss Mayhew right behind her.

"Tekoa—stay here and mind the bread!" Miss Frye

settled a stern eye on the girl. Then quickly she followed her guests out the door, and found them standing in a circle around Sarah.

"So it's you!" thundered Mrs. Stiggins. "You—who can't get a word out of your lips."

"Except to the binnacle boy," said Miss Mayhew.

"And small wonder that your jaws seized shut," Mrs. Stiggins peered into her eyes. "With a secret like yours perched on your tongue."

Sarah lowered her gaze at once and fingered her long, brown hair.

"Namely," Mrs. Stiggins proclaimed, "that it was you who murdered the *Orion*'s crew!"

Sarah's eyes opened wide in terror.

"You couldn't bear your sweetheart Simeon Sprigg forsaking you for the sea." Mrs. Stiggins poked the girl's shoe with the tip of her parasol. "So you poisoned him—and his mates as well!"

Speechlessly, Sarah shook her head, desperately denying the charge. Her jaws trembled, her lips twitched. She labored to open her mouth and speak, noticed Miss Frye's eyes upon her—and all of a sudden broke free.

"Seize her!" Mrs. Stiggins screamed.

Panic-stricken, Sarah dashed off, holding the hem of her skirt as she ran.

"She mustn't escape!" Miss Bunch cried out, and the four took after her in pursuit. Down the middle of the street they scurried, gathering the curious to their cause and shouting for those with fleeter feet to catch the girl at once. Panting, the women turned down an alley, and soon trailed the mob they'd called into being. Along the common, past the graveyard, through a field they hurried along, till they crossed a meadow and at last caught up with the rest of the crowd—at the cliff.

"And where's the girl?" Mrs. Stiggins demanded.

A man turned around. "Sarah Peel, ma'am?"

"Of course! And who else?" Mrs. Stiggins snapped.

"Fell from the cliff, ma'am. Drowned, she did."

Mrs. Stiggins gasped.

Miss Frye closed her eyes.

"Poor, dear Sarah," she whispered.

Side by side, without speaking a word, the women slowly made their way homeward. Left alone for the final block of her journey, Miss Frye cast a glance at the binnacle boy, turned to her left, and approached his ear.

"Sarah spoke truly—he meant to go to sea. Not Simeon Sprigg, but my Ethan."

She paused for a moment. "Sarah must have seen." She licked her lips and drew closer to the statue. "That it was I who poisoned the *Orion*'s crew."

Miss Frye glanced across at her planting of tansy, with whose deadly leaves she'd destroyed her wayward son, and the corrupting crew as well. Dreamily, she stared at the flowers, yellow as the noonday sun—and so failed to notice Tekoa Peel remove her gaze from her mistress' lips, take a step back from the parlor window, and hurry toward the back door.

INVESTIGATING MYSTERIES

This book was set in Janson
and composed by Robin D'Amato.
It was printed on 50 lb. Finch Opaque.
Title page illustration by Rick Geary.

———

Editors: Mary Pearce and
Deborah Jerome-Cohen
Associate Editor: Wendy Murray
Design: Tony DeLuna